Bucolics

Also by Maurice Manning

Lawrence Booth's Book of Visions

A Companion for Owls

Maurice Manning

Bucolics

poems

Harcourt, Inc.

Orlando Austin New York San Diego Toronto London

www.HarcourtBooks.com

Library of Congress Cataloging-in-Publication Data
Manning, Maurice, 1966–
Bucolics/Maurice Manning.—1st ed.
p.   cm.
I. Title
PS3613.A5654B83   2007
811'.6—dc22   2006027182
ISBN 978-0-15-101310-4

Text set in Centaur
Designed by Lauren Rille

Printed in the United States of America
First edition

K J I H G F E D C B A

This book is dedicated to a mother like no other, my own.

Contents

Shepherds are honest people, let them sing.

—George Herbert

I

boss of the grassy green
boss of the silver puddle
how happy is my lot
to tend the green to catch
the water when it rains
to do the doing Boss
the way the sun wakes up
the leaves they yawn a bit
each day a little more
for a tiny reason then
when the leaves outgrow their green
the wind unwinds them Boss
that's the way you go around
if you loose me like a leaf
if you unburden me
if I untaste the taste
of being bossed by you
don't boss me down to dust
may I become a flower
when my blossom Boss is full
boss a bee to my blue lips
that one drop of my bloom
would softly drop into

I

your sweetness once again
if I go round that way
I'll know the doing means
to you what it means to me
a word before all words

II

did you ever have a nickname Boss
a favorite color ever walk around
in a circle for the fun of it do you
snap your fingers hold your breath
do you put things in your pocket
do you notch a stick for every sparrow
is everything a little game to you Boss
a little peekaboo a ring around
the rosy Boss we all fall down that's
the funny part when it happens
do you keep a straight face or do
you laugh what's it like to always know
the answer never have to guess when
you rest do you ever fall asleep

III

the night is trotting toward me Boss
as if you tapped it with a switch
or clicked your tongue against your teeth
it's coming down the pasture soon
I'll hear the leather tackle squeak
I'll see your ankle swinging in
the stirrup Boss you ride the night
but you don't need to hurry no
you've been this way a time or two
before you've hauled your wagon full
of stars it's all old hat for you
you get here when you get here O
I guess you like the same old thing
it's funny but I like it too
I like it when you ride the night
across the sky as if it were
a nag a worn-out horse you don't
mind riding O you get along
your horse is made of silver Boss
it clips like sleep it clops like you

IV

what color is your collar Boss
is your backbone sore from bending over
when you clap your hand against your thigh
does a little cloud of dust fly off
do you wipe your face with your shirttail Boss
I'd bet my wages that you do
though I couldn't say for sure how much
my wages are they're probably
enough O I get by all right
a beech seed here a feather there
a locust wing a wing as light
as air besides it lets light through
I get a double portion from you
I tie my purse strings tight but put
this in your pocket all I have
I'd lay it on the table Boss
for you I'd bet you jerk your lines
you hang your salty harness from
a red nail in your barn you pour
your horse a scoop of oats you give
its tail a tug you say nighty night
you spotted nag it's funny Boss
I can hear you chuckle when

you shut the stall you're happy for
a good day's work a spotted horse
I wonder if that horse's spots are real
or painted on it makes me smile
to think about it Boss even
field hands need a laugh or two
a rusty riddle a twisty tongue
I wouldn't put it past you O
you sneaky devil you cutup Boss

V

you're the hay maker Boss
you light the candle in the sun
dip the water in the rain
O for the whole big picture
you're the painter Boss I know
it's you the biggest boss of all
you must have a sack full of wind
somewhere a barrel full of salt
a recipe for stone things like that
you keep them close to your chest
you keep your secrets Boss
you flash a yellow eye then crow
away you're like a rooster Boss
sometimes you're like a fox

VI

do you get happy Boss do you
get tickled by a funny bird
or doubled over by a tree
a lonesome tree less lonely Boss
because it has a horse beside it
it doesn't matter if the horse
is rubbing anything or not
as long as it's beside the tree
so simple Boss a horse beside
a tree it makes me happy just
to think about two things beside
each other the stick beside the fire
the rock beside the water O
the snow beside the sleepy field
O Boss the moss beside my mouth
when I bend down to say it's me
you mossy bank you happy piece
of green it's me beside you like
a bird I thought I'd let you know
in case you don't have eyes I thought
I'd tell you Boss what always leaves
me happy if you didn't know
already Boss in case you spend
a lot of time beside yourself

VII

do you have a table
Boss do you have
a lantern do you
leave a broom straw
on the mantel when
you blow into your hearth
does it glow Boss
do you touch the broom straw
to the coal do you
touch the lantern next
is that how you make light
like that with little more
than just a breath Boss
what happens next
once your lamp is lit
what happens after that

VIII

O Boss sometimes you take it all
you shuck the corn you slice the pie
in the sky O you're the onliest
the only word that's ever on
my lips I let it slip when I see
the sky lit up like sunshine scattered
on the river though it's nighttime Boss
O all those sparkles all that glimmer
my eyeballs never want to blink
away from you when I know for sure
you're up there making shimmer Boss
you're laying by a little light
for later on I wonder if
you have a wheel to shell the stars
the way you turn the sky I think
your hand is wrapped around a crank

IX

are you ever sorry Boss ever
have a problem ever get
shamefaced stuff your hands
in your big boss pockets
it's never easy is it Boss never
Boss ever get a slow start ever
feel like you're at the end
of the line the end of your rope
have you ever had it up to here
wherever that is on you I know
it's high up to your neck Boss
the top of your head you must
be tall to take it all the way
you do taller than the top
of the moon Boss O I wonder
what you see when you look up

X

you spread the nighttime Boss
all over me you tuck
me in you tuck me tighter
than a splinter in my finger
Boss you breathe a song
into the wind when you get
this close I wish you'd put
your ear against my mouth
so I could tell you something
I could tell you something
Boss if you would just
bend farther down I know
you know what I would say
Boss if you'd put your ear
against my mouth though it
would only be a whisper
I've got a secret Boss
it's burning up my lips

XI

I told that old dog he
could hush Boss I said
there now you're just having
a shaky little dream dream
a dream dream Boss how
about that talking to a dog
that way there there it's just
a little dream dream you
don't have to whimper that's
what I can't stand Boss
to see an old dog whimper
what's in an old dog's dream
dream anyway some rabbits Boss
or barking up a tree say do
you ever have a dream dream
Boss are you running after or
away from me tell me sometime
if your big feet ever twitch

XII

why Boss why do the days drift by
like a leaf asleep on a bed of water
does the leaf forgive the tree that let
it fall into the water does
it know how stiff the river's face
can be how smileless rivers like
to be at least this one Boss not a flinch
or bristle bloomed on its glassy face
the moment the leaf lay down no joy
no breathy gasp from the river's lips
when all the leaf was trying to do
is cuddle Boss does cuddling move
the likes of you are you the river or
the thing that makes the river's face
so still if a thing so little as
a leaf decided to cuddle up
to me I couldn't stand it Boss
I couldn't stare it down like you
I'd have to say you hush now leaf
you hush your little mouth good night

XIII

are you ever in my chest Boss
are you ever in there with a hammer
tapping on my rib cage as if
you want to make a hum drum
right where I can feel it how big
is that little hammer anyway
does it have a silver head Boss
does it spark against my ribs
I know they're made of iron
I've got a heap of horseshoes
nested in my chest like heavy birds
Boss you make them sing you tap
away is one arm bigger than the other
from all that hammering you do
I wonder if you're knocking for
a reason are you just fooling Boss
or have you found a little door
O if it's really you I wish
you'd whistle through the keyhole Boss
I wish you'd lift my little latch

XIV

if you had a feed sack Boss what
would you keep inside a rooster or
a snake do you need to carry things
around I wonder if you hold
a rooster by his feet a snake
behind its head just think a snake
can't carry anything is that
a shame or is it all right Boss
the way things are is just the way
things are it's neither good nor bad
is that what I'm supposed to think
it doesn't matter if you have
a feed sack Boss not one whit to me
you can carry what you want the way
I carry on I wear myself
to pieces but that's just what I mean
O everything gets carried Boss
even if it never moves
I wonder if you ever notice
but sometimes Boss I carry you

XV

how big is your hand Boss hold it up
to show me if you can I need
to know you know I need to know
so many things I think you have
the answer is there one that's big
O Boss a little word to say
it's all okay I'd say your hand
is bigger than the sky I like
a little thought like that do you
the little things add up you know
O everywhere I go you're there
before me Boss you let me tag
along you're like a firefly in
the moon glow always on the spot
tell me if you ever whistle
if you ever get the willies Boss
goosebumps on your elbows if
you ever ask yourself a question

XVI

the light inside the shadow how
it hovers there it's like an owl song
a quiver hoot it shakes a little Boss
I think your face is in that flicker
is your neck a candlewick your face
a flame on top you're always almost
going out so dim sometimes bright Boss
not for the life of me can I put
my finger on it the way it comes
it also goes which is quickly Boss
if you would just sit still I'd carve
your face into a stick then I
could see you Boss a hundred times
a day we could listen for the owl
if he let out a hoot I'd turn
your wooden ear into the wind

XVII

I like the weaving bees I like
the purple clover blossoms the way
the pasture runs away I like
in winter sinking lambs in straw
how I like bearing buckets full
of water waking up the sun
I like making up a little song
O looking at the sky I close
one eye I hold my hand in the air
I let the red hawk tip my fingers
every day I pretend I am
a tree in your pasture Boss a tree
that holds one season underneath
its shade the season of hello
to everything that's still or stirs
because it is the only one

XVIII

there was a fox Boss in my dream
last night a fox the color of
the field before it wakes to green
I didn't know there was a fox
about until it moved until
it moved like it was sliding Boss
it slid across a furrow then
I barely saw it sliding to
the woods sliding to the river Boss
I never know what's going to cross
my path O never what will make
me ask another question that's
a question in itself I'd like
to know why everything is stuck
in the middle Boss of something else
why the fox was stuck inside my dream
though it was making for the river
do you make nothing Boss but questions
did you set that fox inside my head
did you lay that field behind my eyes

XIX

you swirl the dirt like nobody's business
Boss you put me in the middle
in the middle of that dirty swirl
that twirling chimney top you stir
the little cloud it rises then
it falls away you turn me like
a you know what a wagon wheel
I like the turning feeling Boss
you treat me like a hub my hoe
is like a spoke but you're the one
who turns O you're a rounder Boss
you lay your finger on the rim
you give the wheel a spin I know
you're always turning something up
no matter what you turn you make
it want to rise a little swirl
of me a little swirl of dust
is everything a wheel to you
does everything you touch go up

XX

I've got butterflies Boss
all over but mainly on
my hands two butterflies
with blue wings on each hand
they lift my hands they make
me raise my arms they have
a reason Boss I think
they're fussing over me
they drag me underneath
the sun as if the sun
could be a yellow eye
the day's eye Boss I feel
it burning on my neck
you treat me like a flower
Boss you make me lean
if I could look the day
right in the eye without
blinking O Boss would I
see you are you a daisy
the plainest in the field
you common flower Boss
I doubt you give a rip
you even boss the ditch

XXI

you make it all seem easy Boss
the green plus everything to do
with green like sticks which once upon
a time were green before they fell
upon the ground as sticks but sticks
make nests no doubt about it nests
make birds so Boss I think it's fair
to say that birds must come from green
like horses Boss or pastures come
from dirt with green together O
you're smarter than a whip you must
have made good marks your schoolhouse Boss
I wonder if it had a bell

XXII

yes I've tried to hide my face
behind a tree I have been glad
to see the river run with mud
so fast it will not hold my look
but believe me Boss I can not hide
I can not muddy you I can
not chop you from my stony field
you're like a weed you've got yourself
a common name but a name I can't
forget a name like honey Boss
you pour it in my ear you pour
it in my mouth you make me say
it Boss your name it's like a bird
that's come to roost upon my lips
no matter what it will not stir
it sings a single note sometimes
it's just a whisper others it's
a shout it doesn't matter how
I feel about it what I want
from you is nothing Boss compared
to what you want from me you want
it all to always go your way

though I could give you daisies you
would just as soon have weeds if it
were in your favor Boss I guess
you'd prize a briar for its thorns

XXIII

did you pull yourself up by your bootstraps Boss
did you live pillar to post for years
upon years did you make do with what
you had however little it might
have been a pinch of salt between
your fingers a pouch of nothing tied
to a stick did you tote that stick across
your shoulder O I'd swear you did
you had a humble raising up
just like the moon a little at
a time a little bit that's all
I need from you I only need
a pinch of what you've got besides
that's all you ever give I'd make
an oath you live on air alone
you're like a rooster Boss if you
had just one feather left you'd strut
around the barnyard still you just
can't get above your raising Boss
now that makes two of us the way
you spring from nothing nothing Boss
I wonder if you hatched yourself

XXIV

I'm sure you've got a sweet spot
in your pocket Boss a hidey-hole
somewhere do you keep a marble there
do you ever roll that marble around
to see how it rolls do you ever set
it in the crook of your finger do
you shoot it with your thumb O once
in a while I cup my ear to hear
your big thumb snapping Boss I see
your marble rolling through the sky
it's straighter than a walking stick
you show off Boss you think you're slick
you think you're funny ha ha but
I know a sweet spot in the river
a honey hole or two that's where
the silver fishies go to school
you guessed it Boss a fish eye looks
a little like a marble that's
a hook I have on you if one
of us is fishy Boss it's you

XXV

I guess you've got a lot
of hands though I'm just one
of many Boss I'll turn
the dirt I'll shock the corn
O Boss whatever else
you need I'll pitch it in
I'm just another hand
with a face that's funny Boss
as if my hand had eyes
or something sometimes I
get tickled Boss the way
things are I never know
if you get tickled too
I guess you do from time
to time you've got some kind
of spread some kind of place
for sure whenever I
pick pawpaws Boss I think
of you I think you're like
the blackbird laughing in
the tree you watch me reach

XXVI

you toss the stars like clover seed
you sling them through the sky you must
be glad to be a sower Boss
you sow so many things besides
the sky you sow the seed of dew
the seed of night you let it grow
until the morning overgrows
the night when morning blooms you sow
the song that springs from the mouths of birds
a chatter song a single note
you plant them both I know you set
the whistle in the wind you weave
the waves into the grass you bind
the honey to the suckle Boss
you sow the sticky stuff that sticks
the honey to the yellow belly
of the bee but then O green-thumbed Boss
you save a seed for me you sow
it in the furrow of my eye
as if seedtime Boss is a little bit
like sleep I think inside my eye
you keep a little patch of green

XXVII

that bare branch that branch made black
by the rain the silver raindrop
hanging from the black branch
Boss I like that black branch
I like that shiny raindrop Boss
tell me if I'm wrong but it makes
me think you're looking right
at me now isn't that a lark for me
to think you look that way
upside down like a tree frog
Boss I'm not surprised at all
I wouldn't doubt it for
a minute you're always up
to something I'll say one thing
you're all right all right you are
even when you're hanging Boss

XXVIII

the two of us we're cut
from the same cloth Boss
though I am just a thread
compared to you O you
can do it all you raise
the wool up on the sheep
you put the cotton in
the patch I'm just a string
on the spindle Boss that's all
I'll ever be when I
see water running from
a rock I think you must
be down there in the ground
you're a workhorse Boss like me
you work the pump I work
the bucket fair enough
we're tough as leather Boss
tough as nails we go
together don't we the way
nip goes with tuck we grin
we bear it Boss O does
that ever cross your mind

XXIX

boss of the blue sky boss
of green water boss of rain
with thunder out in front of it
boss of the flatland bottoming
the hill O Boss you've got
a hundred marvels underneath
your belt so tight you'll have to poke
another hole if you keep bossing
you boss so much you couldn't take
on something else or could you Boss
I guess you could you're good at bossing Boss
you'll keep on being Boss boss of this
boss of that you're not swelled up
with pride you're just a boss
whenever I see the shadow of
your straw hat Boss I get
back at it I know you Boss
you even boss your shade

XXX

you move in every direction
at once you're worse than
the wind Boss worse than
a rock dropped in the water
here there everywhere that's you
you're like the sunshine always
reaching does it make you happy
Boss you must have fun the way
you dillydally in the grass
from blade to blade I hear
you laughing I hear you clap
your hands I see what happens
next blackbirds hit the air
the treetops wave good-bye you've got
it made you've got it easy Boss
you leave me in stitches how you spin
the stars with just a finger

XXXI

did you teach the woodpecker how
to knock its head against the wood
of hollow trees did you say this
is how you do it Boss then knock
your own boss head so hard into
the tree it made a rattle clap
I'm thinking nine is the number of times
the bird must knock the tree to make
it rattle right does that sound right
to you is nine the number Boss
to make a rattle clap it sounds
all right to me the number sounds
just right inside the rattle Boss
did you teach birds to count did you
teach me to count what counts beyond
the numbers up above them Boss
are you a number or a sound
or something else I can't learn how
to think about you birdbrain Boss
you rattle me you knock me down

XXXII

the birds the bugs even the trees Boss
everybody thought I was a goner
when I was only resting in the field
I wonder what I looked like then
a warm stone waiting for the wind
that's what happens isn't it Boss you
make everything smoother whether
it wants to go that way or not you're
the level path the head of rivers
the hammer that pounds things
down to thinness you drag away
the guessing game Boss I'm glad as I
can be O make me just another layer
if you like today I felt your swing
your leveling I know it's all the same
to you I could see it Boss today my eye
was like a marble balanced on a stick

XXXIII

when you push the clouds so close together Boss
I think you're stuffing sheep into a chute
I think you're giving up O Boss I think
you're winding down your clock how could you Boss
how could you give such white eyes to the clouds
how could you make them 'fraidy cats when all
they are is heavy air well guess what Boss
I get heavy too I drag my feet I don't want
to help you cull the little clouds or run
the big ones down O Boss why can't they have
another place why can't you put a hollow
in the sky why can't you hide your heavy hand
I know it when you're mad you stomp your feet
I wonder Boss what's gotten into you

XXXIV

the river looks so level Boss
it makes me run my hand across
it what you do with water it's
a sight to my poor eyes a sight
like nothing else I'm nothing but
a tadpole Boss compared to you
I'm only fit for shallows but
your pull is like a heavy stone
you'd pull me under if you had
the chance you know the current Boss
the way you know your steady hand
as if you've walked one furrow Boss
a hundred years or so your plow
is bigger than mine I feel its drag
I shudder in the shadow of
your mule your single-gaited beast

XXXV

is that you Boss is that
you hooting in the hollow
are you a night bird Boss
is that your face behind
the moon is that your hand
cupped to the cricket's ear
do you tell the cricket how
to sing do you say that's it
now softer softer now
you little bug do you
pour moonlight on the river
do you say river let
this silver ride on you
you're up to something Boss
you're like a treetop there
against the sky a wave
you're like a neighbor Boss
is your favorite word hello
your favorite game a game
of peep-eye Boss are you
as sweet as you can be
you cutie-pie I can't
keep track of you Boss you're just

too many things at once
you're like a lullaby
that never ends a breath
that makes the moment last
again again again

XXXVI

of course I like the sun
I like it tapping on
my back it makes me turn
I like it lighting up
the horse's breath I turn
to see it every time
it happens Boss you make
it happen all the time
not every day of course
but often just enough
for me I know if you're
not lighting something up
you're doing something else
like pushing birds across
the sky I turn to see
them too whenever you
get pushy Boss you push
the birds you light the horse
you make me turn my face
for you of course of course

XXXVII

do you have a busy season Boss
a season when the apples fall
do you whisper to your bees do you
say one more time make honey please
how many bushels of corn do you
lay by how many is enough
to see you through the winter now
when you hang the sun ball lower in
the sky it glows like a pumpkin Boss
its vine has dropped away its leaves
have curled to sleep I know it's time
for me to lay things by to put
things up for fallow days O Boss
is there ever such a thing a day
when nothing happens nothing moves
I think some days are quiet Boss
that's all no bees no scrape of leaves
but that won't keep the day from humming
do you know my favorite winter tale
I laid a wet lamb in a barrel
I put my coat around it Boss
I hummed it through the night that night

I learned one thing about you Boss
you never stop even in the winter
you're putting up you're laying by
you're dripping hums between my lips

XXXVIII

I'm happy Boss happy as a bird
hopping on a branch just a little branch
on one of your little trees that's all
it takes for me no wage no deeds
just the day-in day-out same old thing
it's okay by me you keep the sun
on its string that's all I need that's
enough for me but also water O
every breath I draw I make
a little picture Boss a little bird
with a whistle in its bones hopping
on a branch like there's no tomorrow
no end in sight you might even say
every day is like the day before

XXXIX

did you boss the horse against the barn
to cut the wind in two or spare
the horse from being all alone
the way you boss the hawk away
from being bored by sending it
the wind you hold the hawk you lay
it all against my eye as if
it were a picture in my head
you make me see belonging Boss
for what it is the thing that holds
it all together like a string
that's tied to everything a loop
that passes from the water to
the bucket Boss the windmill to
the breeze the branch that's swaying from
the hawk that left it for the wind
which lifts the hawk to see the horse
beside the barn one thing about
your string I find surprising Boss
it never has a tangle no
it never has a knot I think
you hold the running end above
the clouds above my seeing once

in a blue moon Boss I think you raise
your finger to give the string a pluck
which makes me happy Boss because
I know a picture never moves
O Boss I think you know it too

XL

is there another sky besides
the blue one Boss another one
that wouldn't just as soon be gray
is there another yellow moon
besides the one that shows its face
so shortly Boss before it turns
it back again as if it sways
from glowing glee then suddenly
its face is pinched to gloom because
a notion dawns upon it Boss
it is the only moon alone
to waver in the only sky
O single-handed boss of all
the only things including me
what reason can you give me now
for filling half of every thing
with honey just to leave the half
remaining torn from even hope
for sweetness like a rabbit's lip
no doubt you run your finger down
the little face of every thing
to cleave it clean in two I'm like

the moon pinned to the only sky
I don't mind rising half the time
the other half I am ashamed
for ever thinking that I could

XLI

the field is flatter than
a table Boss smoother
than a plowshare I've dug
the rocks I've dragged
the heavy log around
I've ironed it out all right
not a wrinkle in sight O
isn't that enough Boss
doesn't everything look nice
look at me I've got a bowl
a wooden cup I'm as ready
as I'll ever be Boss hurry up
you can be the slowest poke
you old molasses boss

XLII

unless my nose is itchy Boss
I think I smell the smell of rain
I see the ring around the moon
it means one thing a rain from you
is coming soon which suits me fine
we sorely need it Boss we being
me the tree O every blade
of grass the creatures all the bugs
even the horseflies need a drink
I'm waiting Boss beside my stack
of little rocks I've got a string
of yellow feathers tied around
my neck that way you'll know it's me
who needs the rain the pokeweed all
the flowers parched for water Boss
O everyone is ready now
I know you have a pond behind
the sun take up your bucket Boss
dip it in the water pour it down
the sky O pour it on the horse
the barn the field the tree the dog
rain on the woolly lambs O lay
a little rain on everything
O tip your bucket Boss this way

XLIII

if I say I've sprung the spring in my step
does it matter Boss does it matter much
to you when I can't even spit
without it feeling bad when I
can't look the old horse in the face
without a tear on mine because
I know where all days go when they
are done they don't come back they won't
wake up the sun won't show its face
again which means there isn't much
to look at Boss not much to look
at in the dark not even you
you keep a lot of secrets Boss
but now I know a secret too
although the tallest tree may reach
your chin I know one day you'll bend
it over Boss without a speck
of pity not a moment's pause
you'll drag it to the darkest ground
all days go one direction down

XLIV

I wonder Boss in all
your days if ever you
have watched a vine like this
unwinding from its branch
unwinding on its own
the vine undoing all
the winding it has done
what makes a vine undo
its winding Boss I thought
the reason for a vine
was winding I like that kind
of reason a little one
unwinding Boss must be
a little bigger say
do you agree are you
the boss of winding or
unwinding Boss or both
whichever one you boss
don't let me get unwound
from you if I unwind
myself I hope you'll turn
your branch against me Boss

XLV

before my eye was burning like
an ember in my head you made
the tree you let the tree see light
before me early light the tree
learned how to hold it so when I
saw light the light was roosted in
the tree on every shining leaf
too many candles Boss to count
but I am sure how many wicks
there were among them only one
you must have touched it once with your
hot finger Boss you let it glow
until you wet your fingers then
you gave the wick a pinch I can't
explain you Boss why you take light
away though now I give the tree
a second light the light is less
I know it Boss it burns me now
to smell the smoke like burnt light shook
right from the burning tree is this
the kind of light you might call last
will I smell smoke before you shake
the light from me before you pinch
my little flame into a hiss

XLVI

the way that buzzard hops it makes
me sad to see him Boss the way
he flops around I know his wings
won't work he's got a naked tail
a tail as naked as the moon
that floppy buzzard Boss is like
the moon if you could drive a nail
into it do you know what I mean
it isn't going anywhere
but only you would dare to raise
your hammer to the moon you keep
the fledglings on the ground I know
he's just a busybody Boss
another nosy nose who can't
leave well enough alone that's what
that wobbly buzzard is alone
he's come to me a pauper Boss
without a feather to my name
what makes him think that I can trick
the air that I know how to fly

XLVII

I put my face against
the horse's shoulder Boss
I breathed into the frost
so white upon his coat
I saw the patch I left
a darker spot as dark
as darkness gets I let
the horse cut through the field
the spot was looking out
an empty eye unblinking
unblinking Boss which one
of us was that supposed
to be O was it you
so steady Boss or was
that patch of empty me

XLVIII

when I chop wood you warm me twice
you send a wind then send the cool
behind it Boss we work together
side by side when I drop the share
in the dirt you make it sing you give
a song to turning dirt we keep
some big irons in the fire don't we
Boss we keep it stoked there's wood
in the wood box there's a kettle on
the stove there's a whisper coming from
the kettle whenever something's doing
there's always something else that's just
the way it is side by side Boss
just like I said O one plus one
is too as in also Boss always
also O one thing also then
another that's the way you are
the way you always are I think
your favorite number Boss is two

XLIX

O boss of ashes boss of dust
you bother with what floats above
the chimney what settles to the ground
you wake the motes from sleep you make
them curtsy in a ray of sun
they hold their tiny breath as if
they're waiting for the little name
of the dance that's coming next then they
will take their places Boss if I
were smaller I would join them O
I'd cut a rug or two I'd slap
my hand against my shoe if that's
the kind of fuss you're raising Boss
you know I never know for sure
I only know you bother me
from time to time you've caught my breath
a time or two you've stirred me up
before which makes me want to tell
you Boss I wouldn't mind it if
you bothered me a little more

L

I've got a picture of you Boss
a picture on the slate in my head
that never goes away two feet
two hands that's what I see I bet
you've got a bedbug or two
a rolly polly curled up in
your hand O everybody says
you've got a beard clear down to there
but I believe you're baby faced
Boss a face as smooth as an onion
nor not one set of shoes beneath
your bed you old barefooter Boss
you old-timer you can't pull my leg
O I was born in the nighttime Boss
you know the story nothing fancy
like you when you were little Boss
did you make mud pies play with crickets
did you tie feathers in your hair

LI

I got up early Boss the moon
was still a hand above the line
I mean the line below the sky
so perfect Boss so straight a line
it never wavers never wakes
up early just like you know who
for just a moment Boss the moon
held steady on that line you might
say like a breath held in a mouth
a big mouth Boss but also like
a funny little horse who waits
for just one reason O to run
away when I get close the truth
is you're the one who runs from me
I'm hobbled Boss I never move
at all just look at you you're strung
so high the way you run away
I ought to tie you to a tree

LII

your other favorite word
is not a word at all
you get so hushed up Boss
my ears get lonely I wish
you'd let me hear from you
sometime I wonder what
you're up to Boss up there
up there you won't leave up
alone whatever you
put up it stays even
if it's heavy Boss though it
is thinner than a silk
of corn your upper lip
is like an anvil Boss
you wouldn't move it if
it itched there's so much weight
behind it resting on
your tongue that tongue you keep
stuck to the roof of your mouth
you've got the upper hand
all right though you won't brag
about it now there's one

more thing your favorite word
the first one that's the one
you never told me Boss

LIII

I'm like an oak tree Boss O
I'm coming down with something
I'm coming down with something
in my middle in the middle where
my little rings grow Boss
the wind could push me over
what else can I say I see
your pasture Boss your rise
you boss it all you boss the wind
you boss the trees I wish
you'd boss me back Boss
boss back the wind so I
won't lean so far over Boss
I'm tired of leaving too O
boss the leaves back on my branches
boss the birds back to my arms
Boss tell them I'm not falling Boss

LIV

you windy blowhard Boss
you could peel the hoops
right off a barrel you
could leave the lonely staves
to topple over what
would be the name to call
the barrel then a used-
to-be a has-been Boss
I say it looks more changed
than broken I can see
its wooden ribs the curve
it cut into the air
so long ago it's just
a shadow it won't catch
a drop of rain but it's
a wonder just the same
a barrel living long
although the hoops it wore
like collars Boss are gone
it swells me just to look
but I'm not fooled by you
you haven't given up
your craft your vessel trade

it always comes around
to you somehow I know
your hands are always full
you barrel-making fool
you stretch yourself too thin
for your own good unless
for mine I'm collared Boss
for you to pass the task
of making hoops to me

LV

do you put your trousers on one leg
at a time like me or do you just snap
your fingers Boss you fancy-pants
you think you're special just because
you keep a tighter rein on the sun
because you're dimming down the day
a little sooner now you know
how to paint a green leaf red without
me seeing you O every day
you make me glad though I wish sometimes
you'd stop it Boss I wish you'd cut
it out the way you muddy up
the water you're like a dirty fish
you always get away which makes
me think you wear a cloud instead
of trousers now I know behind
that cloud you've got your fingers crossed
you're hiding something Boss don't fool
with me is it a reason or
a riddle I'm getting tired of all
your games I've had it up to here
O Boss I've had enough of you

LVI

are you against me Boss
the way a yellow leaf
holds down the patch of dirt
beneath it as if the dirt
could raise itself from dirt
what other purpose could
it have you lay the leaf
against the ground to keep
the ground from thinking so
you hush it up you make
it mind its beeswax Boss
what weight a yellow leaf
could measure if it had
your heavy hand behind
it Boss you go against
the grain I feel your hand
on me as heavy as
a hay bale though lighter than
a shadow Boss you hold
me down you hold me back
you push against me O
I hope you're happy now

LVII

say what have you got underneath
your floppy hat anyway Boss
besides your head a piece of string
a play pretty thing perhaps
a lucky feather do you even
need luck a little charm I doubt
it Boss since you've already got
the numbers at least the ones that count
you know the raindrops in the river
the blackbirds rising in the sky
how that sky looks like it's waving Boss
a hundred little waves in one
even now it carries me away
never ever could I count that high
O underneath your hat is nothing
but a tree a little tree whose leaves
have pictures colored on them one
of which I hope is me my tree
my horse my little dog my field
O Boss underneath my leaf
isn't there a rule for crickets when
they rub their legs together Boss
they tip your hat a little bit
whatever else they do they lift

LVIII

guess what Boss I'm not even
tired not even blinking hardly
even after all the sunup-to-sundown
sweat on my brow save the end
of daylight I could keep on working
Boss there's nothing now to do
but let the dewdrops drop the way
they do when the day is done what a life
Boss one day to me must be nothing
but a speck to you older than dirt
I guess is it okay if I pretend
I see your fingers bent around the moon
as if your hand is right behind it
something like that Boss that's what
I do when I can't sleep a wink I think
about you Boss I wonder all those yellow
fireflies even though they never make
a peep do they still call you Boss

LIX

when I see the shadow of the hawk
but not the hawk itself do you know
what it feels like Boss a stone a stone
set on my chest it weighs me down
it's stronger than the horse's strain
against the plow lines Boss it's like
the river after rain I can't
hold back the pull the pull that makes
me like its heft I even like
the shadow's tiny yoke O Boss
I feel its curve around my neck
I see a flap of wings so black
it binds me to the furrows Boss
a shadow smarter than the sting
of a switch though it is lighter than
a feather though it is thinner than
a leaf that shadow stone is one
of many wonders Boss for all
the world it makes me think of you
you heavy thing you never move

LX

can I say whew to you now Boss
can I say Boss I'm tuckered out
I'm at the end of the row for sure
can I say I've had enough of these
long days when you hang the sun so high
so long I want to give the hoe
a rest I worry that I'll wear
the handle out but deep down Boss
I know the hoe is never tired
it never needs to sleep or pass
the day just sitting in the shade
you made the hoe so straight I can't
chop down its purpose Boss it's good
for one thing only nothing else
I wonder is that all I am
to you am I that simple Boss
is there a handle in my head
have you fetched me from your giant shed

LXI

you let out light to tease the shadows
they rollick underneath the tree
they tear each other up they wear
each other out some days are like
a horse upended wallowing
in a little patch of dust a sign
the horse is happy Boss for sure
it's tickled to its tickle bone
all right a laughing stock but Boss
not every day is funny no
today's a day that's lifted but
tomorrow might be dragging down
again a day when branches droop
a day when shadows leave the light
alone when the horse is serious
when nothing whinnies nothing neighs
whenever there's a to I know
a fro is coming after it
is that a kind of tickle too
is there a tickle bone between
two days that hang together like
a hinge is there a reason why

I think you're making fun of me
a reason why I like it Boss
you sender of the sun you rain
for rivers all those leaves you bend

LXII

listen Boss don't think that I
don't like my corn-shuck bed
my oak-stump stool don't
think I mind the empty sky
everything is fine fine
as a frog hair split down
the middle Boss finer than
a dandelion's beard I need
to know why even little lambs
kneel down to the grass
their knees turn green O Boss
I need to know about these
lovely things they're something else
I have so many questions Boss
I can't keep count just once
I wish you'd tell me why

LXIII

my hay day Boss is every day
the wonder of it never ends
never goes away I never fail
to breathe the sun the summer season
even in the winter even
if the horse's breath is blowing blue
as smoke each time I turn the fork
each time I hear the ring of tines
each time they turn more silver Boss
I taste a long day on my tongue
it's always sweet it's always more
than just a chore I've learned a thing
or two from pitching hay one thing
about the hay it's more than kindling
in the belly of the horse's stove
the second thing beyond the hay
this time about the fork I've made
its handle shiny from my hands
around its throat so shiny now
it's like a mirror Boss it's like
a glass in which I see your face
your burning eye about to wink

LXIV

if I didn't know you better Boss
I'd say you're overlooking me
because I've seen your shoulder Boss
the one that gives me shivers so
much like a stone it never moves
I can't get over you I can't
undo the part of you that hates
to blink so much it makes me think
you look away you lead-face Boss
you're like a tree that doesn't care
to wave good-bye to the last leaf of
the season when it tumbles down
the dizzy air a leaf without
a name that's me a tree without
a shrug or shame that's you but I
know better Boss there's nothing lead
about you O I've got you pegged
you're like dewdrops puddled on a rock
I touch it Boss it quivers then
I see the open sky asleep
it's sleeping on your silver eye
I pick you up I put my hands
around you Boss I know my face

won't fit inside the scene there's so
much nothing Boss it makes me think
there's nothing to it but listen now
I'm looking over you so if
I told you I was thirsty would
you shrink I wonder Boss if all
at once I swallowed you O tell
the truth how would that grab you Boss

LXV

the first hawk you hung up in the sky
Boss O tell me did you give
it any warning any sign
that something fun was going to happen
I wonder if you said listen Red
I'm going to let you ride the wind
you won't even have to flap
Boss how many days ago was that
I'd say it was a lot a lot
of hawks a lot of days it's always
a lot of everything with you
you big britches Boss you do just what
you want to do I guess you think
it's cute to hang a little hawk
you're full of surprises Boss you keep
me on my toes how many times
will I go tippy toe for you
you boss of all the good stuff boss
of all the numbers hang me Boss
you make me wish I was a bird

LXVI

you know that little song
I whistle Boss I only know
a little bit but I like it just
the same the same song all
the time Boss I don't care
it sounds fine to me it feels like
a clover button in my teeth
sweet sweet as the morning
Boss every morning is a morning
do you ever think about that
everything that stays the same
like rain like grass like you
you're always Boss boss
of the morning boss of my whistle
O boss of my little song

LXVII

it doesn't bother me Boss to have
a boss like you so always on
my back you don't let up you won't
back down from what you want to be
my boss no I don't mind it Boss
I couldn't boss myself too well
I couldn't even try I need
someone to tell me what to do
someone to say let's fetch the hoe
let's cap that post with a rock we'll keep
it dry up top as if we're side
by side as if you've got a row
you're working Boss as if you've got
a hoe I never see I'd like
to hear it sing at least I'd say
it makes a pretty song why keep
it to yourself why hush it up
you hushed-up Boss you're so much like
a post you make me sigh two feet
stuck in the ground head bone poked
above the sky a dandy cut
from the straightest stretch of the hardest tree
you'd think a post would have a lot
to say O how it doesn't Boss

LXVIII

is your barn stuffed to the roof beam
with reasons Boss or sheaves of things
you want to happen bundled up
like stalks of wheat by your tally
is your loft bursting at the seams
is there no chaff for you to thresh
no floor to leave the threshings on
no cinder heap to burn your doubts
if I could trace the marks you've made
behind the little tracks the bird
leaves planted in the snow if I
could find the little ladder Boss
that's leaning straight against the sky
how many rungs would I have to climb
before I reached your hand would you
be spinning out another yarn
a new one on your wheel would you
be hatching something else to say
would I see doodles curling through
the pages of your ledger Boss
would I see glistening before
your face two fingers blazed with ink

LXIX

beyond the field this time
he's back once more the fox
beyond my doings Boss
beyond my little day
my stack of wood the curl
of smoke my chimney makes
the little bit of what
I do for you so small
it hardly matters O
I know it all adds up
but I won't ever reach
that fox he's up there Boss
he's up there like a leaf
that isn't leaving until
I see it well I see
it Boss as red as blood
so red it makes me pale
beside it but I'm glad
he's back because for just
a moment Boss I know
he matters more than me
he matters more than you
for just a moment then

the moment goes away
just like the way you wash
the sky when it turns red
for shame or sorrow I
don't know you never leave
it very long I guess
you've got your reasons well
I guess that's why you're Boss

LXX

would you trade hee-haws with a crow
would you ever sit back Boss to let
a crow go gitchy goo on you
those crows they're always cutting up
the air not one of them could sing
without a cackle in his song
it's hard to call a song it's such
a ha-ha Boss if crows had teeth
I think they'd blind me with their smile
you know they're always making fun
of something O they even laugh
at rain if they had hands they'd slap
their thighbones half in two if they
could slap would it be hard for them
to do it only once O Boss
they laugh so hard it's just as well
they don't have hands it's funny Boss
how smart you are to make a crow
the way you did it it's a joke
it gets me tickled to the quick
O you're so serious it makes
me wonder if your face stays straight
or if once in a rainy season you

don't laugh until your eyes are wet
until you have to fetch the rag from your
back pocket to halt the stream of salt
that's running like a team of horses
across the furrows on your cheeks
as if you were ashamed or shy
to let on you were smiling Boss

LXXI

does an old dog toll beside you Boss
when you walk fences when you cut
across a field how many feet
are rustling through the grass at once
I wonder if the number six
rings a bell for you do you need
to be reminded Boss of all
your goings-on your doings how
no matter what the old dog's tail
is like a tongue against your thigh
it never fails to strike do you
forget these things don't tell me I
already know the answer Boss
remember is your middle name
you've got a mind like a trap a stick
stuck under a wooden box you pull
the string you spring the snare you're not
surprised by what you see in there
inside that box a little field
an old dog pealing at your side
a line of fencing yawning like
a river running out of sight
but far behind you is a shape

that looks like me how funny Boss
for both of us to wind up caught
in your design it happens O
I also have a dog I'm sure
you've heard him howling on your heels
he's sounding out your shadow Boss
what kind of bell is ringing now

LXXII

you leave a little night inside
the flower Boss to keep it closed
although the sun is up above
the middle branches of the tree
the flower has a little night
inside it I can see it Boss
a drop of pitch a pinch of sleep
as if the flower wants the night
to last a little longer than
it does I'm like the flower Boss
sometimes I want the night to last
so I can keep on sleeping when
I'm sleeping I don't have to think
about you Boss it's harder than
a summer field that hasn't seen
the rain for days to think about
you Boss do you know that you stone
you're hard to get around you're like
the morning always there when my
eyes flutter open when they see
the daylight coming softly that's
a laugh a thing so hard it starts
out easy Boss when I wake up
I feel a feather on my face

LXXIII

would you be lonesome if I swam
across the river Boss to cross
the line of trees to another field
so far it's just another line
another line of trees somewhere
another river's line O Boss
sometimes it's all just lines to me
it's always one line leading to
another line how lovely all
the little lines can be you see
I'd like to see the first one Boss
I'd like to see the place where you
invented water then I'd like
to climb the tree that's first to feel
the wind I'd touch the post where you
unhitch the moon at night then hitch
it up again I only know
I'm down the longest line from you
when something lovely happens Boss
I know just where it starts the first
blackbird of morning sings because
you pierce it in the heart O tell

me boss of arrows boss of bows
how many times you reach into
your quiver before your day is done
is it a hundred times or one

LXXIV

we've always been like this
one finger wrapped around
another Boss that close
but I don't need to tell
you anything about it
why you could creep into
a mouse-hole shadow in
the pocket of my pants
without me being wise
to where you are you're such
a sneaky sneak I can't
keep you away away
is where I try to go
sometimes I'm sorry Boss
I do I haven't got
a reason why I go
around around so much
I'm always coming back
around to you O please
believe me do you Boss

LXXV

you raise the hawk you hoist the crows
around it Boss they tip their wings
they lift their voices but the crows
are not afraid how suddenly
the hawk could turn to drive them from
the patch of sky they're riding in
how soon their spat could matter less
than one breath matters to the wind
does any of it matter Boss
to you perhaps that is the king
of questions have you drawn your lips
together for a whistle or
a sigh what happens in the sky
is so beneath you Boss I think
the hawk is one idea one
old look upon his face the same
old stare as stubborn as a post
the crows are like a harrow to
unbroken ground they turn it loose
they give it air the very air
below you Boss that's turning now
with birds such lovely darlings if

the hawk is like the river then
I think the crows are like the rain
how do you feel about it Boss
can you abide this swell this strain

LXXVI

thank you for the leaf Boss
thank you for the tree thank
you for the knife-edge wind
thank you for the breath behind
the wind breath sweeter than
a horse's sweet oat breath
thank you Boss O thank you
for the yellow-belly sun for
the moon fatter than a tick
thank you for the season
thank you for the long-leg
shadows Boss thank you
for paring down the day
today for bossing all of it
away except the fish-eye sky
O except the leaf that leapt
into my hands thank you for
two hands to make a cup
to hold the leaf Boss thank you
for the red bug riding on the leaf

LXXVII

am I your helper Boss or am
I not do I bring in the hay
for me or you or only for
the horse I help the horse he helps
me too why sometimes Boss he hooks
his head across my shoulder just
to rest it there he'll heave a sigh
as if he's tuckered he always makes
me laugh he knows I know he wants
an apple Boss his heavy head
on me it helps it helps so much
it helps to hear him sigh a sigh
he doesn't really mean he means
another thing is that the way
you mean to mean another Boss
another thing beyond the thing
you want from me you see the horse
gives me a weary sigh when he's
not sleepy Boss he doesn't want
to hear sweet dreams from me he wants
to hear you want an apple hoss
I mean we help each other Boss

LXXVIII

I've got one thing to say to you
that's blackberry winter Boss
your little cool spell in the spring
your dewy days so lingering
your fiddling with the sun you slow
the season down you pull the reins
you lay a whoa on everything
as if you want the dawn to last
until the dusk as if you want
to taste the dawn a little longer
O I don't blame you Boss the dawn
is sweet who wouldn't want to hold
it back I like it when you hold
me back I like it when you jerk
the reins I know the gee or haw
if either comes will come from you
but when you let the reins go slack
now that's a different story Boss
I don't like that that moment when
you turn me out alone to graze
to graze is such a hot-faced slight
as close as breath but never close
enough to know if I was hitched

for real or if the hitching Boss
I felt was just a feeling sweet
but not the honeypot itself
which swings the gate right back to you
O tell me why I can't hold back
this bitter thought are you the bee
or just a stinging story Boss

Acknowledgments

Many of these poems originally appeared in the following magazines and journals: *Hunger Mountain, Pool, Shenandoah, The Southeast Review, The Virginia Quarterly Review, Washington Square,* and *Wind.* One of these poems was first published in the anthology *Legitimate Dangers: American Poets of the New Century.* I am thankful to the editors of these publications for their support.

I must also recognize the following people for their friendship and their belief in this book during its long season of growth: Rebecca Howell, Dan Rowland, Davis McCombs, Jake Adam York, David Harwell, Crystal Wilkinson, Keith Nightenhelser, John and Barbara, Rick and Emily, and, as always, the Kentucky Order of Old Regulars. I am especially grateful to André Bernard, Julie Marshall, Michelle Blankenship, David Hough, Jenna Johnson, and the rest of the staff at Harcourt for their wisdom and kindness.